100 Great
POEMS

100 Great

POEMS

Favourite Poems and their Poets
Selected by Victoria Parker
Introduction by Fiona Waters

Miles Kelly
PUBLISHING

First published in 2000 by
Miles Kelly Publishing Ltd
Bardfield Centre, Great Bardfield, Essex CM7 4SL

4 6 8 10 9 7 5

Design
Nicola Witt, Phil Kay

Art Direction
Clare Sleven

Cover Design
Ran Abraham

Artwork commissioned by
Janice Bracken, Susanne Grant, Natasha Smith

Art reference and picture research
Lesley Cartlidge, Liberty Newton

British Library Cataloguing-in-Publication Data
A catalogue record for this book is available from the British Library

ISBN 1 902947 54 1

We thank the following illustrators who provided work for this title:

Vanessa Card; Mark Davis; Nicholas Forder; Chris Forsey; Terry Gabbey/AFA Ltd; Luigi Galante; Roger Gorringe/Illustration Ltd; Peter Gregory; Sally Holmes; Richard Hook/Linden Artists; Barry Jones; Gilly Marklew/SGA Illustrations and Design; Eddie Mooney/SGA Illustrations and Design; Tracey Morgan/B.L.Kearley; Chris Odgers; Linda Richardson; Terry Riley; Mike Saunders; Rob Sheffield; Gwen Tourret/B.L.Kearley; Rudi Vizi; Mike White.

Contact us by email: info@mileskelly.net

Printed in China

Foreword

Poetry can capture a myriad of emotions in one apparently simple phrase. Even those not familiar with a great range of poems will turn to the anthology to find words suitable for that special occasion, be it wedding or funeral. The reading of WH Auden's howl of grief *Stop all the Clocks* was a highly charged moment in the film *Four Weddings and a Funeral*. It revived Auden's popularity, but more importantly poetry became 'cool'. For too long poetry had been regarded as 'difficult' and so ignored. Schools didn't know how to teach it and so rote learning became the norm, with lines of deathless verse repeated over and over with little comprehension and even less pleasure. The end result was often a deep dislike of poetry and a resolve never to open a poetry book again.

If we don't encourage the reading and enjoyment of poetry all we will be left with is a generation who know nothing but advertising jingles and pop song lyrics. Great poetry may well be off-putting to the sound bite generation if it is force fed, but this collection, *100 Great Poems*, offers something for all the family. Ranging from the Bible to Benjamin Zephaniah it puts the modern and the accessible alongside the classical and explains that this is all poetry – and look, it can be understood, it can make you laugh, it can make you cry. The book also accompanies the poems with varied and imaginative illustrations and helpfully provides biographical notes and asides. So poetry assumes its rightful place as part of our wonderful literary heritage, a special part, but not a daunting part.

One winter afternoon when I was about seven I heard *The Lady of Shalott* read on the wireless by Gabriel Woolf. I was hooked for life. *100 Great Poems*, will I am sure, provide just such a hook for many of its readers.

Fiona Waters
Dorset, March 2000

Contents

LOOKING TO HEAVEN

WAR AND HEROISM

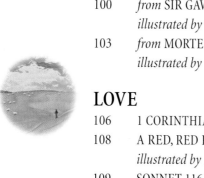

CHRISTMAS

LIFE AND DEATH

HOME AND WORK

The Thought-Fox

I imagine this midnight moment's forest:
Something else is alive
Beside the clock's loneliness
And this blank page where my fingers move.

Through the window I see no star:
Something more near
Though deeper within darkness
Is entering the loneliness:

Cold, delicately as the dark snow
A fox's nose touches twig, leaf;
Two eyes serve a movement, that now
And again now, and now, and now

Sets neat prints into the snow
Between trees, and warily a lame
Shadow lags by stump and in hollow
Of a body that is bold to come

Across clearings, an eye,
A widening deepening greenness,
Brilliantly, concentratedly,
Coming about its own business

Till with a sudden sharp hot stink of fox
It enters the dark hole of the head.
The window is starless still; the clock ticks,
The page is printed.

Ted Hughes

1930–98, b. England

Ted Hughes was appointed Poet Laureate in 1984. He married another of the twentieth century's finest writers, Sylvia Plath. The Thought-Fox explores Hughes's fascination with both animals and the subconscious. The fox is imaginary, but also acutely real. Hughes is so absorbed in observing nature through his mind's eye that the act of writing takes place unnoticed. The two are inextricably linked – even the appearance of the words on the page mirror the fox's footprints in the snow.

Upon Westminster Bridge

Earth has not anything to show more fair:
Dull would he be of soul who could pass by
A sight so touching in its majesty:
This City now doth like a garment wear

The beauty of the morning: silent, bare,
Ships, towers, domes, theatres, and temples lie
Open unto the fields, and to the sky,
All bright and glittering in the smokeless air.

Never did sun more beautifully steep
In his first splendour valley, rock, or hill;
Ne'er saw I, never felt, a calm so deep!

The river glideth at his own sweet will:
Dear God! the very houses seem asleep;
And all that mighty heart is lying still!

William Wordsworth
1770–1850, b. England

Wordsworth is perhaps the 'father of modern poetry', for he was the first poet to make his own feelings and thoughts the subject of his work. He and his best friend, Coleridge, were the first of several poets later grouped together as 'the Romantics'. Wordsworth wrote this poem while crossing Westminster Bridge on a coach to France. According to his notes, the city was transfigured in the dawn light with 'something like the purity of one of nature's own grand spectacles'.

Prelude I

The winter evening settles down
With smell of steaks in passageways.
Six o'clock.
The burnt-out ends of smoky days.
And now a gusty shower wraps
The grimy scraps
Of withered leaves about your feet
And newspapers from vacant lots;
The showers beat
On broken blinds and chimney-pots,
And at the corner of the street
A lonely cab-horse steams and stamps.

And then the lighting of the lamps.

T S Eliot

1888–1965, b. USA

Thomas Stearns Eliot was born in St Louis and educated at Harvard, the Sorbonne, and Oxford. He settled in England due to the encouragement of the poet Ezra Pound. Much of Eliot's work speaks of the disillusionment of the generation who lived through the horrors of World War I. His poems often show European cities as nightmarish places of decay and unreality, and humans as broken, confused wretches for whom life has lost all meaning.

Sea-Fever

I must go down to the seas again, to the lonely sea and the sky,
And all I ask is a tall ship and a star to steer her by,
And the wheel's kick and the wind's song and the white sail's shaking,
And a grey mist on the sea's face and a grey dawn breaking.

I must go down to the seas again, for the call of the running tide
Is a wild call and a clear call that may not be denied;
And all I ask is a windy day with the white clouds flying,
And the flung spray and the blown spume, and the sea-gulls crying.

I must go down to the seas again, to the vagrant gypsy life,
To the gull's way and the whale's way where the wind's like a whetted knife;
And all I ask is a merry yarn from a laughing fellow-rover,
And quiet sleep and a sweet dream when the long trick's over.

John Masefield

1878–1967, b. England

*J*ohn Masefield had a life-long love of the sea. He trained for the merchant navy when he was only 13 years old. However, his first trip (at the age of 16, to Chile) was a disaster as he suffered from terrible seasickness! Sea-Fever was included in his first published book, Salt-Water Ballads (1902). Masefield became Poet Laureate in 1930 and in 1935 he received the Order of Merit.

From a Railway Carriage

Faster than fairies, faster than witches,
Bridges and houses, hedges and ditches;
And charging along like troops in a battle,
All through the meadows the horses and cattle:
All of the sights of the hill and the plain
Fly as thick as driving rain;
And ever again, in the wink of an eye,
Painted stations whistle by.

Here is a child who clambers and scrambles,
All by himself and gathering brambles;
Here is a tramp who stands and gazes;
And there is the green for stringing the daisies!
Here is a cart run away in the road
Lumping along with man and load;
And here is a mill, and there is a river:
Each a glimpse and gone for ever!

Robert Louis Stevenson

1850–94, b. Scotland

Robert Louis Stevenson is best known for his well-loved novels: the adventure stories Treasure Island *(1883) and* Kidnapped *(1886), and* The Strange Case of Dr Jekyll and Mr Hyde *(1886). From a Railway Carriage was published in his first volume of poetry,* A Child's Garden of Verses *(1885). Stevenson suffered from very poor health, and many of the poems in this book were written when he was lying ill in bed in Tahiti, remembering childhood holidays at his grandfather's home.*

I Hear America Singing

I hear America singing, the varied carols I hear,
Those of mechanics, each one singing his
as it should be blithe and strong,
The carpenter singing his
as he measures
his plank or beam,

The mason singing his
as he makes ready for work,
or leaves off work,
The boatman singing what
belongs to him in his boat,
the deckhand singing on the steamboat deck,
The shoemaker singing as he sits
on his bench, the hatter
singing as he stands,

The wood-cutter's song,
the ploughboy's on his way in the morning,
or at noon intermission or at sundown,
The delicious singing of the mother,
or of the young wife at work,
or of the girl sewing or washing,

Each singing what belongs to him
or her and to none else,
The day what belongs to the day –
at night the party of young fellows, robust, friendly,
Singing with open mouths their strong melodious songs.

Walt Whitman
1819–92, b. USA

*W*alt Whitman lived during the 'wild west' – the driving out of the Native Americans, the Gold Rush, the Civil War, the first trans-America railroad, and Custer's 'Last Stand'. Whitman had very little education and he was proud of being a 'working man' like the pioneers. He strove to write about ordinary people in ordinary language, and though he was determined to avoid being 'literary', his first book, Leaves of Grass (1855) has become one of the greatest works of American literature.

Ain't I a Woman?

That man over there say
    a woman needs to be helped into carriages
and lifted over ditches
    and to have the best place everywhere.
Nobody ever helped me into carriages
    or over mud puddles
        or gives me a best place ...

And ain't I a woman?
    Look at me
Look at my arm!
    I have plowed and planted
and gathered into barns
    and no man could head me ...
And ain't I a woman?
    I could work as much
and eat as much as a man –
    when I could get to it –
and bear the lash as well
    and ain't I a woman?
I have borne thirteen children
    and seen most all sold into slavery
and when I cried out a mother's grief
    none but Jesus heard me ...

And ain't I a woman?
 that little man in black there say
a woman can't have as much rights as a man
 cause Christ wasn't a woman
Where did your Christ come from?
 From God and a woman!
Man had nothing to do with him!
 If the first woman God ever made
was strong enough to turn the world
 upside down, all alone
together women ought to be able to turn it
 rightside up again.

Sojourner Truth
1797–1883 b. USA
adapted by Erlene Stetson

Sojourner Truth was born a black female slave when even white free women had few rights. She was freed by the New York Emancipation Act of 1827 and left New York in 1843 with only a bag of clothes and 25 cents. She spent the rest of her life campaigning for the rights of black people and women, and rose to become head councillor of Freedman's village in Virginia. This poem was originally a speech made at the Women's Rights Convention in Ohio, 1852.

In A Station of the Metro

The apparition of these faces in the crowd;
Petals on a wet, black bough.

Ezra Pound

1885–1972, b. USA

*E*zra Pound was a great writer, teacher and critic who founded a poetry movement called Imagism. It shared the aim of traditional Japanese art – to paint wonderful pictures with as few brush strokes as possible. The Imagist poets used language sparingly, chose their words meticulously, and put them together with the greatest attention to rhythm and positioning on the page. In a Station of the Metro is one of the most beautiful and best examples of this type of poem.

A Description of the Morning

Now hardly here and there an hackney-coach

Appearing, showed the ruddy morn's approach.

Now Betty from her Master's bed had flown,

And softly stole to discompose her own.

The slipshod 'Prentice from his Master's door,

Had pared the street, and sprinkled round the floor.

Now Moll had whirled her mop with dextrous airs,

Prepared to scrub the entry and the stairs.

The Youth with broomy stumps began to trace

The kennel edge, where wheels had worn the place.

The Smallcoal-man was heard with cadence deep,

Till drowned in shriller notes of Chimney-sweep.

Duns at his Lordship's gate began to meet;

And Brickdust Moll had screamed through half a street.

The Turnkey now his flock returning sees,

Duly let out a-nights to steal for fees.

The watchful Bailiffs take their silent stands;

And Schoolboys lag with satchels in their hands.

Jonathan Swift

1667–1745, b. Eire

Jonathan Swift was a priest who became deeply involved with Irish-Anglo politics. He travelled from Ireland to London several times, meeting with the top politicians of the day, and writing many political pamphlets. A Description of the Morning, a picture of life in London, was penned as light relief from his serious works and appeared in The Tatler. Swift published nearly all his work anonymously and received payment for only one, the classic Gulliver's Travels (1726) – a fee of £200.

from The Odyssey

Thus, near the gates conferring as they drew,
Argus, the dog, his ancient master knew;
He, not unconscious of the voice and tread,
Lifts to the sound his ear, and rears his head.
Bred by Ulysses, nourished at his board,
But ah, not fated long to please his lord!
To him, his swiftness and his strength were vain;
The voice of glory called him o'er the main.
Till then in every sylvan chase renowned,
With Argus, Argus, rung the woods around;
With him the youth pursued the goat or fawn,
Or traced the mazy leveret o'er the lawn.
Now left to man's ingratitude he lay,
Unhoused, neglected, in the public way,
And where on heaps the rich manure was spread,
Obscene with reptiles, took his sordid bed.

He knew his lord; he knew, and strove to meet,
In vain he strove to crawl, and kiss his feet;
Yet – all he could – his tail, his ears, his eyes
Salute his master, and confess his joys.
Soft pity touched the mighty master's soul;
Adown his cheek a tear unbidden stole,
Stole unperceived; he turned his head, and dried
The drop humane, then thus impassioned cried:

'What noble beast in this abandoned state
Lies here all helpless at Ulysses' gate?

*   *   *

The dog, whom fate had granted to behold
His lord, when twenty tedious years had rolled,
Takes a last look, and having seen him, dies;
So closed for ever faithful Argus' eyes!

Homer *circa 725–675 BC*
translated by Alexander Pope
1688–1744, b. England

The Odyssey, *like* The Iliad, *is traditionally attributed to a mysterious poet called Homer, although it is now suspected that each poem had a different writer. Both epics draw from the saga of the Trojan war, but while* The Iliad *focuses on the fighting,* The Odyssey *tells of the warrior king Odysseus's long and dangerous journey home. Alexander Pope wrote many widely-acclaimed poems and essays of his own, but it was his Homeric translations that brought him fame and fortune.*

Poem

As the cat
climbed over
the top of

the jamcloset
first the right
forefoot

carefully
then the hind
stepped down

into the pit of
the empty
flowerpot

William Carlos Williams

1883–1963, b. USA

William Carlos Williams was a New Jersey pediatrician whose patients were often from the poorest and lowliest walks of life. He strove to capture in his poetry the simple, stark essence of the people, objects, events, and emotions that he observed while going about his surgeries and house calls. Williams is a master of showing ordinary things in a fresh way – often with tenderness and compassion.

Things Men Have Made –

Things men have made with wakened hands, and put soft life into
are awake through years with transferred touch, and go on glowing
for long years.
And for this reason, some old things are lovely
warm still with the life of forgotten men who made them.

D H Lawrence

1885-1930, b. England

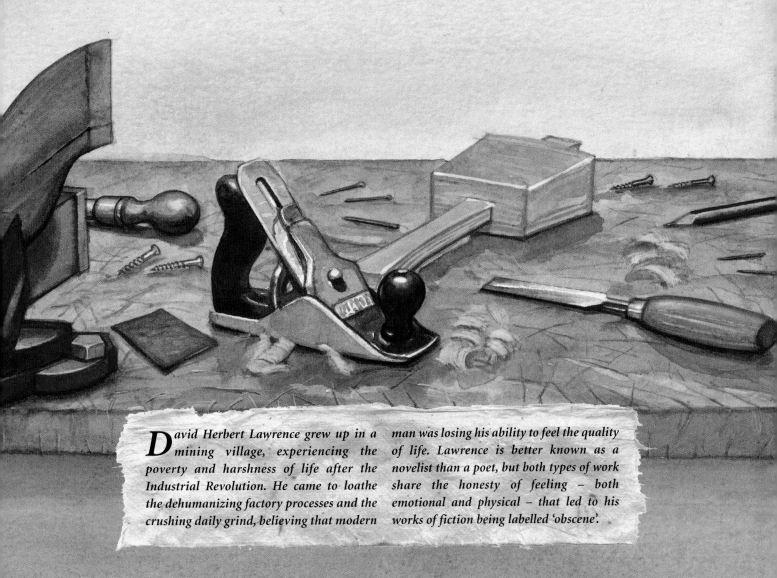

David Herbert Lawrence grew up in a mining village, experiencing the poverty and harshness of life after the Industrial Revolution. He came to loathe the dehumanizing factory processes and the crushing daily grind, believing that modern man was losing his ability to feel the quality of life. Lawrence is better known as a novelist than a poet, but both types of work share the honesty of feeling – both emotional and physical – that led to his works of fiction being labelled 'obscene'.

Blacksmiths

Swarthy smoke-blackened smiths, smudged with soot,
Drive me to death with the din of their banging.
Men never knew such a noise at night!
Such clattering and clanging, such clamour of scoundrels!
Crabbed and crooked, they cry, 'Coal! Coal!'
And blow with their bellows till their brains burst.
'Huff! Puff!' pants one: 'Haff! Paff!' another.
They spit and they sprawl and they spin many yarns.
They grate and grind their teeth, and groan together,
Hot with the heaving of their hard hammers.
Aprons they have, of hide of the bull,
And greaves as leg-guards against glowing sparks.
Heavy hammers they have, and hit hard with them;
Sturdy strokes they strike on their steel anvils.
Lus, bus! Las, bas! they beat in turn –
Such a doleful sin, may the Devil destroy it!
The smith stretches a scrap, strikes a smaller,
Twines the two together, and tinkles a treble note:
Tik, tak! Hic, hac! Tiket, taket! Tyk, tak!
Bus, lus! Bas, las! Such a life they lead,
These Dobbin-dressers: Christ doom them to misery!
There's no rest at night for the noise of their water-fizzing.

Anon
circa 1425–50
translated from Medieval English by Brian Stone

*T*his medieval poem is a highly accomplished example of the tradition of alliterative verse that existed in England before the Norman conquest and enjoyed a revival at the time of Chaucer (circa 1343–1400). The style fits the subject perfectly – the clashing consonants brilliantly evoke the clanging of blacksmiths at work. However, the poem is unique for its shortness; other alliterative poems (such as **Sir Gawain and the Green Knight**) are much longer.

Night Mail

(Commentary for a GPO Film)

I
This is the Night Mail crossing the Border,
Bringing the cheque and the postal order,

Letters for the rich, letters for the poor,
The shop at the corner, the girl next door.

Pulling up Beattock, a steady climb:
The gradient's against her, but she's on time.

Past cotton-grass and moorland boulder,
Shovelling white steam over her shoulder,

Snorting noisily, she passes
Silent miles of wind-bent grasses.

Birds turn their heads as she approaches,
Stare from bushes at her blank-faced coaches.

Sheep-dogs cannot turn her course;
They slumber on with paws across.

In the farm she passes no one wakes,
But a jug in a bedroom gently shakes.

II

Dawn freshens. Her climb is done.

Down towards Glasgow she descends,

Towards the steam tugs yelping down a glade of cranes,

Towards the fields of apparatus, the furnaces

Set on the dark plain like gigantic chessmen.

All Scotland waits for her:

In dark glens, beside pale-green lochs,

Men long for news.

III

Letters of thanks, letters from banks,

Letters of joy from girl and boy,

Receipted bills and invitations

To inspect new stock or to visit relations,

And applications for situations,

And timid lovers' declarations,

And gossip, gossip from all the nations,

News circumstantial, news financial,

Letters with holiday snaps to enlarge in,

Letters with faces scrawled on the margin,

Letters from uncles, cousins and aunts,

Letters to Scotland from the South of France,

Letters of condolence to Highlands and Lowlands,

Written on paper of every hue,

The pink, the violet, the white and the blue,

The chatty, the catty, the boring, the adoring,

The cold and official and the heart's outpouring,

Clever, stupid, short and long,

The typed and the printed and the spelt all wrong.

IV

Thousands are still asleep,

Dreaming of terrifying monsters

Or a friendly tea beside the band in Cranston's or Crawford's:

Asleep in working Glasgow, asleep in well-set Edinburgh,

Asleep in granite Aberdeen,

They continue their dreams,

But shall wake soon and hope for letters,

And none will hear the postman's knock

Without a quickening of the heart.

For who can bear to feel himself forgotten?

W H Auden

1907–73, b. England

Wystan Hugh Auden's first volume of poems was published when he was only 23 years old by T S Eliot, who was then a Director of Faber & Faber. In 1927, the first talking movie was made in America and the 'golden age' of film began. Auden worked with the GPO film unit from 1935, and Night Mail was written as an accompaniment to a cinema show-reel. Through his work with the GPO, Auden came to know the composer Benjamin Britten, who set many of his poems to music.

DISTANT LANDS

Ozymandias

I met a traveller from an antique land
Who said: Two vast and trunkless legs of stone
Stand in the desert . . . Near them, on the sand,
Half sunk, a shattered visage lies, whose frown,
And wrinkled lip, and sneer of cold command,
Tell that its sculptor well those passions read
Which yet survive, stamped on these lifeless things,
The hand that mocked them and the heart that fed;
And on the pedestal these words appear:
'My name is OZYMANDIAS, king of kings:
Look on my works, ye Mighty, and despair!'
Nothing beside remains. Round the decay
Of that colossal wreck, boundless and bare
The lone and level sands stretch far away.

Percy Bysshe Shelley
1792–1822, b. England

Bullied as a boy, Shelley grew up to ignore social convention. He dressed unusually; was vegetarian and atheist; eloped with a 16 year-old, then left her for Mary Godwin (author of Frankenstein). Twice he tried to set up a community of 'free spirits'. Ozymandias describes how a dictator's efforts to be remembered forever have been beaten by time and nature. (Ozymandias was another name for the Egyptian Pharaoh Rameses II, who built a huge tomb in the shape of a Sphinx.)

The Soldier

If I should die, think only this of me:
  That there's some corner of a foreign field
That is for ever England. There shall be
  In that rich earth a richer dust concealed;
A dust whom England bore, shaped, made aware,
  Gave, once her flowers to love, her ways to roam,
A body of England's, breathing English air,
  Washed by the rivers, blessed by the suns of home.

And think, this heart, all evil shed away,
  A pulse in the eternal mind, no less
   Gives somewhere back the thoughts by England given;
Her sights and sounds; dreams happy as her day;
  And laughter, learnt of friends; and gentleness,
   In hearts a peace, under an English heaven.

Rupert Brooke

1887–1915, b. England

Rupert Brooke served in the RNVR during World War I. After taking part in the Antwerp expedition of 1914, he wrote The Soldier *as one of five 'War Sonnets'. The poems were published early in 1915 in* New Numbers *and were given a rapturous reception by the public. Brooke died of blood poisoning the same year, on a French hospital ship in the Aegean Sea, and the posthumous publication of 1914 and* Other Poems *firmly established him as the nation's poet of war.*

Kubla Khan

In Xanadu did Kubla Khan
A stately pleasure-dome decree:
Where Alph, the sacred river, ran
Through caverns measureless to man
    Down to a sunless sea.
So twice five miles of fertile ground
With walls and towers were girdled round:
And here were gardens bright with sinuous rills,
Where blossomed many an incense-bearing tree;
And here were forests ancient as the hills,
Enfolding sunny spots of greenery.

But oh! that deep romantic chasm which slanted
Down the green hill athwart a cedarn cover!
A savage place! as holy and enchanted
As e'er beneath a waning moon was haunted
By woman wailing for her demon-lover!
And from this chasm, with ceaseless turmoil seething,
As if this earth in fast thick pants were breathing,
A mighty fountain momently was forced:
Amid whose swift half-intermitted burst
Huge fragments vaulted like rebounding hail,
Or chaffy grain beneath the thresher's flail:
And 'mid these dancing rocks at once and ever

It flung up momently the sacred river.
Five miles meandering with a mazy motion
Through wood and dale the sacred river ran,
Then reached the caverns measureless to man,
And sank in tumult to a lifeless ocean:
And 'mid this tumult Kubla heard from far
Ancestral voices prophesying war!

The shadow of the dome of pleasure
Floated midway on the waves;
Where was heard the mingled measure
From the fountain and the caves.
It was a miracle of rare device,
A sunny pleasure-dome with caves of ice!

A damsel with a dulcimer
In a vision once I saw:
It was an Abyssinian maid,
And on her dulcimer she played,
Singing of Mount Abora,
Could I revive within me
Her symphony and song,

To such a deep delight 'twould win me,
That with music loud and long,
I would build that dome in air,
That sunny dome! those caves of ice!
And all who heard should see them there,
And all should cry, Beware! Beware!
His flashing eyes, his floating hair!
Weave a circle round him thrice,
And close your eyes with holy dread,
For he on honey-dew hath fed,
And drunk the milk of Paradise.

Samuel Taylor Coleridge

1772–1834, b. England

Samuel Taylor Coleridge lived to see many amazing scientific discoveries and also the French Revolution, when the ordinary people overthrew the ruling nobility. It must have seemed as if anything was possible if only you had enough imagination and energy. Kubla Khan describes a man who imagines paradise on Earth and tries to turn it into reality. But Coleridge said that even he wasn't sure what the poem really meant. According to him, he dreamed the lines during a nap!

Home-Thoughts, from Abroad

O to be in England
Now that April's there,
And whoever wakes in England
Sees, some morning, unaware,
That the lowest boughs and the brushwood sheaf
Round the elm-tree bole are in tiny leaf,
While the chaffinch sings on the orchard bough
In England – now!

And after April, when May follows,
And the whitethroat builds, and all the swallows!
Hark, where my blossom'd pear-tree in the hedge
Leans to the field and scatters on the clover
Blossoms and dewdrops – at the bent spray's edge –
That's the wise thrush; he sings each song twice over
Lest you should think he never could recapture
The first fine careless rapture!
And though the fields look rough with hoary dew,
All will be gay when noontide wakes anew
The buttercups, the little children's dower
– Far brighter than this gaudy melon-flower!

Robert Browning
1812–89, b. England

*R*obert Browning spent much of his childhood reading in his father's massive library of 6,000 books, and wrote his first volume of poems at the age of 12. He had limited success early on in his career, and after trips to Russia and Italy, he eloped to Italy in 1846 with the poet Elizabeth Barratt. The couple lived first in Pisa, then in Florence, Browning only returning home to England after Elizabeth's death in 1861.

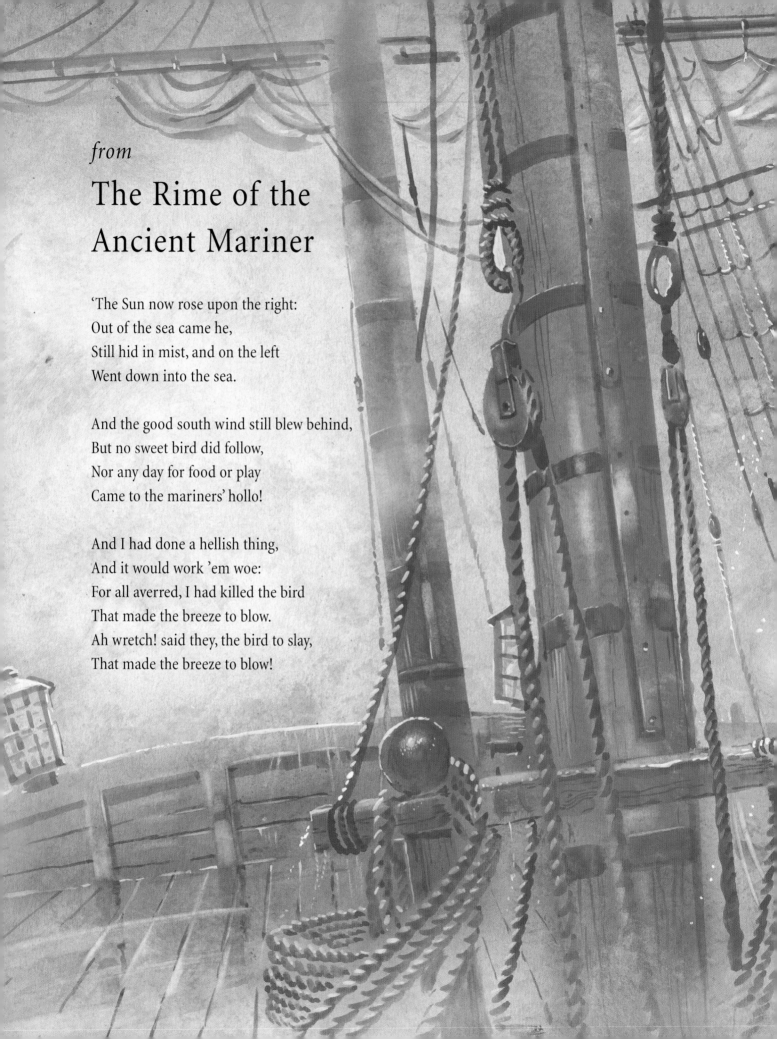

from

The Rime of the Ancient Mariner

'The Sun now rose upon the right:
Out of the sea came he,
Still hid in mist, and on the left
Went down into the sea.

And the good south wind still blew behind,
But no sweet bird did follow,
Nor any day for food or play
Came to the mariners' hollo!

And I had done a hellish thing,
And it would work 'em woe:
For all averred, I had killed the bird
That made the breeze to blow.
Ah wretch! said they, the bird to slay,
That made the breeze to blow!

* * *

Down dropt the breeze, the sails dropt down,
'Twas sad as sad could be;
And we did speak only to break
The silence of the sea!

All in a hot and copper sky,
The bloody Sun, at noon,
Right up above the mast did stand,
No bigger than the Moon.

Day after day, day after day,
We stuck, nor breath nor motion;
As idle as a painted ship
Upon a painted ocean.

Water, water, every where,
And all the boards did shrink;
Water, water every where,
Nor any drop to drink.

The very deep did rot: O Christ!
That ever this should be!
Yea, slimy things did crawl with legs
Upon the slimy sea.

About, about, in reel and rout
The death-fires danced at night;
The water, like a witch's oils,
Burnt green and blue and white.

And some in dreams assurèd were
Of the Spirit that plagued us so;
Nine fathom deep he had followed us
From the land of mist and snow.

And every tongue, through utter drought,
Was withered at the root;
We could not speak, no more than if
We had been choked with soot.

Ah! well a-day! What evil looks
Had I from old and young!
Instead of the cross, the Albatross
About my neck was hung.'

Samuel Taylor Coleridge
1772–1834, b. England

*T*his great Romantic poem tells the story of an old sea-dog, whose ship once got ice-bound near the South Pole. An albatross appears and the ship floats free, but when the sailor shoots the bird, a curse falls upon the vessel and it is becalmed under the burning Equator sun. A skeleton ship approaches and all the crew die except the narrator. It is only when the mariner finds the kindness to bless the slimy watersnakes in the rotting sea, that the ship is finally able to turn for home.

NATURE

Daffodils

I wander'd lonely as a cloud
That floats on high o'er vales and hills,
When all at once I saw a crowd,
A host of golden daffodils,
Beside the lake, beneath the trees
Fluttering and dancing in the breeze.

Continuous as the stars that shine
And twinkle on the milky way,
They stretch'd in never-ending line
Along the margin of a bay:
Ten thousand saw I at a glance
Tossing their heads in sprightly dance.

The waves beside them danced, but they
Out-did the sparkling waves in glee: –
A Poet could not but be gay
In such a jocund company!
I gazed – and gazed – but little thought
What wealth the show to me had brought.

For oft, when on my couch I lie
In vacant or in pensive mood,
They flash upon that inward eye
Which is the bliss of solitude;
And then my heart with pleasure fills
And dances with the daffodils.

William Wordsworth

1770–1850, b. England

Wordsworth grew up in the wild beauty of Cumbria. After travelling to Italy and France, he lived in Dorset and Somerset, before returning to his beloved Lake District. Many of his poems describe uplifting moments of joy that suddenly came upon him when he was on his own amidst nature. The sense of peace and permanence he experienced in the natural world were proof to him that all things – even human poverty and tragedy – were part of a harmonious creation.

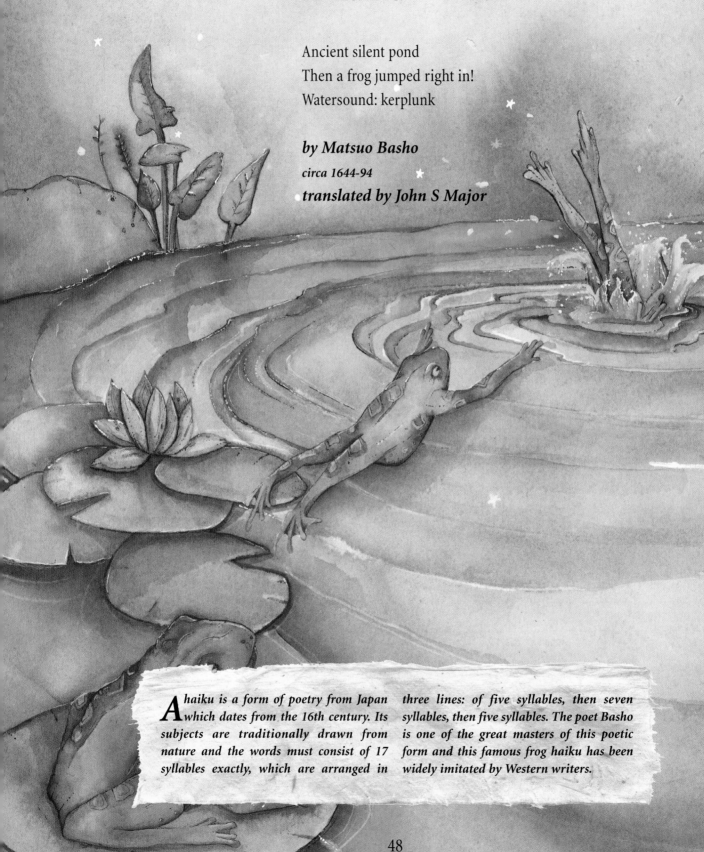

A haiku

Ancient silent pond
Then a frog jumped right in!
Watersound: kerplunk

by Matsuo Basho
circa 1644-94
translated by John S Major

A haiku is a form of poetry from Japan which dates from the 16th century. Its subjects are traditionally drawn from nature and the words must consist of 17 syllables exactly, which are arranged in three lines: of five syllables, then seven syllables, then five syllables. The poet Basho is one of the great masters of this poetic form and this famous frog haiku has been widely imitated by Western writers.

from The Song of Hiawatha

At the door on summer evenings
Sat the little Hiawatha;
Heard the whispering of the pine-trees,
Heard the lapping of the water,
Sounds of music, words of wonder;
'Minne-wawa!' said the pine-trees,
'Mudway-aushka!' said the water.

Saw the firefly, Wah-wah-taysee,
Flitting through the dusk of evening,
With the twinkle of its candle
Lighting up the brakes and bushes;
And he sang the song of children,
Sang the song Nokomis taught him:
'Wah-wah-taysee, little firefly,
Little, flitting, white-fire insect,
Little, dancing, white-fire creature,
Light me with your little candle,
Ere upon my bed I lay me,
Ere in sleep I close my eyelids!'

Henry Wadsworth Longfellow
1807–82, b. USA

There was once a real Hiawatha (he lived in the 15th century and was chief of the Onondaga tribe of Iroquois Native Americans), and his heroic achievements have become the magical stuff of legend.

Longfellow's The Song of Hiawatha (1858) popularized the folklore of the original inhabitants of America. Longfellow is the only American to be honoured with a bust in the Poets' Corner of Westminster Abbey.

from Dover Beach

The sea is calm to-night.
The tide is full, the moon lies fair
Upon the straits; – on the French coast the light
Gleams and is gone; the cliffs of England stand,
Glimmering and vast, out in the tranquil bay.
Come to the window, sweet is the night-air!
Only, from the long line of spray
Where the sea meets the moon-blanched land,
Listen! you hear the grating roar
Of pebbles which the waves draw back, and fling,
At their return, up the high strand,
Begin, and cease, and then again begin,
With tremulous cadence slow, and bring
The eternal note of sadness in.

Matthew Arnold

1822–88, b. England

Part of **Dover Beach** dates from Matthew Arnold's honeymoon, when he stayed at Dover. He was a Schools Inspector by profession, who travelled extensively throughout England for 15 years and campaigned for improved education and social conditions. After writing several volumes of poetry, Arnold turned in later life to writing critical essays, becoming the leading critic of his day.

King of Carrion

His palace is of skulls.

His crown is the last splinters
Of the vessel of life.

His throne is the scaffold of bones, the hanged thing's
Rack and final stretcher.

His robe is the black of the last blood.

His kingdom is empty –

The empty world, from which the last cry
Flapped hugely, hopelessly away
Into the blindness and dumbness and deafness of the gulf

Returning, shrunk, silent

To reign over silence.

Ted Hughes
1930–98, b. England

King of Carrion *comes from* Crow *(1970), a sequence of poems partly inspired by a meeting with the American artist Leonard Baskin, who ultimately illustrated much of Ted Hughes's poetry.* *Characteristically of Hughes, the* Crow *poems are brutal and violent. The bird symbolizes a chaotic, indestructible force in a primeval world, where death is lord over nature.*

from Endymion

A thing of beauty is a joy for ever:
Its loveliness increases; it will never
Pass into nothingness, but still will keep
A bower quiet for us, and a sleep
Full of sweet dreams, and health, and quiet breathing.
Therefore, on every morrow, are we wreathing
A flowery band to bind us to the earth,
Spite of despondence, of the inhuman dearth
Of noble natures, of the gloomy days,
Of all the unhealthy and o'er-darkened ways
Made for our searching – yes, in spite of all,
Some shape of beauty moves away the pall
From our dark spirits. Such the sun, the moon,
Trees, old and young, sprouting a shady boon
For simple sheep; and such are daffodils
With the green world they live in; and clear rills
That for themselves a cooling covert make
'Gainst the hot season; the mid-forest brake,
Rich with a sprinkling of fair musk-rose blooms;
And such too is the grandeur of the dooms
We have imagined for the mighty dead,
All lovely tales that we have heard or read –
An endless fountain of immortal drink,
Pouring unto us from the heaven's brink.

John Keats
1795–1822, b. England

*J*ohn Keats is regarded as one of the main poets of the Romantic movement. Endymion (pub. 1818) was his longest work, and tells the Greek legend of a shepherd called Endymion who falls in love with the goddess Cynthia. The poem was originally slammed by the critic Lockhart as 'drivelling idiocy'! Keats was deeply hurt, but wrote courageously, 'I think I shall be among the English poets after my death'.

The Windhover

To Christ Our Lord

I caught this morning morning's minion, kingdom
    of daylight's dauphin, dapple-dawn-drawn Falcon, in his riding
    Of the rolling level underneath him steady air, and striding
High there, how he rung upon the rein of a wimpling wing
In his ecstasy! then off, off forth on swing,
    As a skate's heel sweeps smooth on a bow-bend; the hurl and gliding
    Rebuffed the big wind. My heart in hiding
Stirred for a bird, – the achieve of, the mastery of the thing!

Brute beauty and valour and act, oh, air, pride, plume, here
    Buckle! AND the fire that breaks from thee then, a billion
Times told lovelier, more dangerous, O my chevalier!

    No wonder of it: shèer plòd makes plough down sillion
Shine, and blue-bleak embers, ah my dear,
    Fall, gall themselves, and gash gold-vermilion.

Gerard Manley Hopkins

1844–89, b. England

Hopkins was a priest who struggled to reconcile his acute sense of God's hand in nature with the religious doctrine that the natural world is fallen. Here, a soaring windhover resembles Christ on the cross. Hopkins marvels at the bird's mastery of the air, but finds it is the moment when the wind overcomes the bird that is the most magnificent. Earth is most beautiful when broken by the plough, and embers when they disintegrate. For Hopkins, nature is reflecting the glory of Christ's death.

Silver

Slowly, silently, now the moon
Walks the night in her silver shoon;
This way, and that, she peers, and sees
Silver fruit upon silver trees;
One by one the casements catch
Her beams beneath the silvery thatch;
Couched in his kennel, like a log,
With paws of silver sleeps the dog;
From their shadowy cote the white breasts peep
Of doves in a silver-feathered sleep;
A harvest mouse goes scampering by,
With silver claws, and silver eye;
And moveless fish in the water gleam,
By silver reeds in a silver stream.

Walter de la Mare
1873–1956, b. England

Walter de la Mare worked as a book keeper until 1908, when he was granted a Civil List pension. However, he was a life-long writer and began to contribute poems and stories to magazines when he was in his mid-twenties. He also wrote novels. A modest and gentle man, he at first wrote under an assumed name, Walter Ramal, which is part of his real name spelt backwards!

To Autumn

Season of mists and mellow fruitfulness,
    Close bosom-friend of the maturing sun;
Conspiring with him how to load and bless
    With fruit the vines that round the thatch-eaves run;
To bend with apples the mossed cottage-trees,
    And fill all fruit with ripeness to the core;
        To swell the gourd, and plump the hazel shells
    With a sweet kernel; to set budding more,
And still more, later flowers for the bees,
Until they think warm days will never cease,
    For Summer has o'er-brimmed their clammy cells.

Who hath not seen thee oft amid thy store?
    Sometimes whoever seeks abroad may find
Thee sitting careless on a granary floor.
    Thy hair soft-lifted by the winnowing wind;
Or on a half-reaped furrow sound asleep.
    Drowsed with the fume of poppies, while thy hook
        Spares the next swath and all its twinèd flowers:
    And sometimes like a gleaner thou dost keep
Steady thy laden head across a brook;
Or by a cider-press, with patient look,
    Thou watchest the last oozings, hours by hours.

Where are the songs of Spring? Ay, where are they?

Think not of them, thou hast thy music too –

While barrèd clouds bloom the soft-dying day,

And touch the stubble-plains with rosy hue;

Then in a wailful choir the small gnats mourn

Among the river sallows, borne aloft

Or sinking as the light wind lives or dies;

And full-grown lambs loud bleat from hilly bourn;

Hedge-crickets sing; and now with treble soft

The red-breast whistles from a garden croft;

And gathering swallows twitter in the skies.

John Keats

1795–1822, b. England

Keats abandoned his apothecary's licence at 21 years old for poetry. However, he composed his greatest poems in just one year of his writing career, at a time when he was beset by financial problems and ill health! Beginning in Sept. 1818, Keats wrote: **The Eve of St Agnes,** *his famous* **Odes, La Belle Dame sans Merci,** *and* **Lamia,** *among others.* **To Autumn** *was Keats's last major poem, written Sept. 1819. It celebrates the abundance of the season and mourns the passing of summer.*

'A Slash of Blue'

A slash of Blue –
A sweep of Gray –
Some scarlet patches on the way,
Compose an Evening Sky –
A little purple – slipped between
Some Ruby Trousers hurried on –
A Wave of Gold –
A Bank of Day –
This just makes out the Morning Sky.

Emily Dickinson
1830–86, b. USA

From a distinguished family and educated at a foremost women's college, Emily Dickinson shut herself inside her house for increasing periods until eventually she wouldn't leave home at all and refused to see nearly everybody. After her death, her sister found a box containing almost 2,000 poems – some in carefully hand-stiched books, others scrawled onto scraps. They were finally published and Emily Dickinson is now considered to be one of the greatest American poets.

Full Moon and Little Frieda

A cool small evening shrunk to a dog bark and the clank
of a bucket –

And you listening.
A spider's web, tense for the dew's touch.
A pail lifted, still and brimming – mirror
To tempt a first star to a tremor.

Cows are going home in the lane there, looping the hedges
with their warm wreaths of breath –
A dark river of blood, many boulders,
Balancing unspilled milk.

'Moon!' you cry suddenly, 'Moon! Moon!'

The moon has stepped back like an artist gazing amazed
at a work
That points at him amazed.

Ted Hughes
1930–98, b. England

Ted Hughes's lifelong fascination with animals and the natural world began in childhood with the many shooting and fishing trips he enjoyed with his brother. This poem from Wodwo (1967) captures a moment when a small child suddenly feels and understands something huge in nature. Her experience of the world is creating who she is, just as an artist creates a work of art. (Ted Hughes's and Sylvia Plath's daughter, Frieda, was born in 1960.)

The Tyger

Tyger! Tyger! burning bright
In the forests of the night,
What immortal hand or eye
Could frame thy fearful symmetry?

In what distant deeps or skies
Burnt the fire of thine eyes?
On what wings dare he aspire?
What the hand dare seize the fire?

And what shoulder, & what art,
Could twist the sinews of thy heart?
And when thy heart began to beat,
What dread hand? & what dread feet?

What the hammer? what the chain?
In what furnace was thy brain?
What the anvil? what dread grasp
Dare its deadly terrors clasp?

When the stars threw down their spears,
And water'd heaven with their tears,
Did he smile his work to see?
Did he who made the Lamb make thee?

Tyger! Tyger! burning bright
In the forests of the night,
What immortal hand or eye,
Dare frame thy fearful symmetry?

William Blake

1757–1827, b. England

William Blake worked as an engraver all his life and strove to be thought of as an artist rather than a poet. His first collection of poems was published in 1784, and the second – Songs of Innocence (1789) – he wrote, illustrated, engraved, printed, and sold all himself. Blake was an independent thinker who rebelled against authority and developed a highly unorthodox, visionary interpretation of Christianity. The Tyger *appeared in* Songs of Experience (1794).

A Birthday

My heart is like a singing bird
    Whose nest is in a watered shoot:
My heart is like an apple-tree
    Whose boughs are bent with thickset fruit;
My heart is like a rainbow shell
    That paddles in a halcyon sea;
My heart is gladder than all these
    Because my love is come to me.

Raise me a dais of silk and down;
    Hang it with vair and purple dyes;
Carve it in doves and pomegranates,
    And peacocks with a hundred eyes;
Work it in gold and silver grapes,
    In leaves and silver fleurs-de-lys;
Because the birthday of my life
    Is come, my love is come to me.

Christina Rossetti

1830-94, b. England

Christina Rossetti's family were devoted to literature, music and art. Christina composed poetry from an early age and frequently modelled for her painter brother, Dante Gabriel Rossetti. Her 'nursery rhymes,' verses, ballads, and sonnets are often haunted by a wistful melancholy. The overwhelming joy expressed in **A Birthday** suggests that, while it can be read as either a devotional or a secular poem, it was more likely intended as an expression of Christina's devout religious faith.

The Oxen

1. Christmas Eve, and twelve of the clock.
　　'Now they are all on their knees,'
　An elder said as we sat in a flock
　　By the embers in hearthside ease.

2. We pictured the meek mild creatures where
　　They dwelt in their strawy pen,
　Nor did it occur to one of us there
　　To doubt they were kneeling then.

3. So fair a fancy few would weave
　　In these years! Yet, I feel,
　If someone said on Christmas Eve,
　　'Come; see the oxen kneel,

4. 'In the lonely barton by yonder coomb
　　Our childhood used to know,'
　I should go with him in the gloom,
　　Hoping it might be so.

Thomas Hardy

1840–1928, b. England

An architect by trade, Thomas Hardy made his fame and fortune as a novelist. However, he always wrote poetry too, believing it to be superior to fiction. When Tess of the D'Urbervilles (1891) and Jude the Obscure (1895) caused outrage, Hardy gave up writing novels and concentrated on his poems. Many remember cherished moments in the past, often associated with his first wife. The Oxen is a tender memory of the strong religious faith of his childhood.

from The Wreck of the Deutschland

On Saturday sailed from Bremen,
American-outward-bound,
Take settler and seamen, tell men with women,
Two hundred souls in the round –
O Father, not under thy feathers nor ever as guessing
The goal was a shoal, of a fourth the doom to be drowned;
Yet did the dark side of the bay of thy blessing
Not vault them, the million of rounds of thy mercy not reeve even them in?

Into the snows she sweeps,
Hurling the haven behind,
The Deutschland, on Sunday; and so the sky keeps,
For the infinite air is unkind,
And the sea flint-flake, black-backed in the regular blow,
Sitting Eastnortheast, in cursed quarter, the wind;
Wiry and white-fiery and whirlwind-swivellèd snow
Spins to the widow-making unchilding unfathering deeps.

She drove in the dark to leeward,
She struck – not a reef or a rock
But the combs of a smother of sand: night drew her
Dead to the Kentish Knock;
And she beat the bank down with her bows and the ride of her keel;
The breakers rolled on her beam with ruinous shock;
And canvas and compass, the whorl and the wheel
Idle for ever to waft her or wind her with, these she endured.

Hope had grown grey hairs,
Hope had mourning on,
Trenched with tears, carved with cares,
Hope was twelve hours gone;
And frightful a nightfall folded rueful a day
Nor rescue, only rocket and lightship, shone,
And lives at last were washing away:
To the shrouds they took, – they shook in the hurling and horrible airs.

One stirred from the rigging to save
The wild woman-kind below,
With a rope's end round the man, handy and brave –
He was pitched to his death at a blow,
For all his dreadnought breast and braids of thew:
They could tell him for hours, dandled the to and fro
Through the cobbled foam-fleece. What could he do
With the burl of the fountains of air, buck and the flood of the wave?

They fought with God's cold –
And they could not and fell to the deck
(Crushed them) or water (and drowned them) or rolled
With the sea-romp over the wreck,
Night roared, with the heart-break hearing a heart-broke rabble,
The woman's wailing, the crying of child without check –
Till a lionness arose breasting the babble,
A prophetess towered in the tumult, a virginal tongue told.

*   *   *

Sister, a sister calling

A master, her master and mine! –

And the inboard seas run swirling and hawling;

The rash smart sloggering brine

Blinds her; but she that weather sees one thing, one;

Has one fetch in her: she rears herself to divine

Ears, and the call of the tall nun

To the men in the tops and the tackle rode over the storm's brawling.

Gerard Manley Hopkins

1844–89, b. England

Only Hopkins's closest friends knew during his lifetime that he was a poet. Now he is famous for his bold and creative use of language and rhythm. This poem was inspired by the loss of The Deutschland in December 1875, whose passengers included five Franciscan nuns exiled from Germany for their faith. Hopkins grapples with the question of how God can allow tragedy and human suffering, and finds the answer in Christ's own pain and sacrifice – success is often through 'failure'.

On His Blindness

When I consider how my light is spent,
    Ere half my days, in this dark world and wide,
    And that one talent which is death to hide,
    Lodged with me useless, though my soul more bent
To serve therewith my Maker, and present
    My true account, lest he returning chide,
    'Doth God exact day-labour, light denied?'
    I fondly ask. But Patience, to prevent
That murmur, soon replies: 'God doth not need
    Either man's work or his own gifts; who best
    Bear his mild yoke, they serve him best. His state
Is kingly: thousands at his bidding speed,
    And post o'er land and ocean without rest;
    They also serve who only stand and wait.'

John Milton

1608-74, b. England

A highly accomplished Classical scholar, if John Milton hadn't been a poet, he would have been a clergyman. He campaigned tirelessly for many years in a highly volatile political arena for the defence of religious and civil liberties. He became aware of his failing sight during the Civil War, and was completely blind by the age of 42. Milton wrote most of his great poetry after this, composing it in his head and dictating it aloud to a secretary.

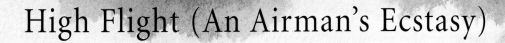

High Flight (An Airman's Ecstasy)

Oh, I have slipped the surly bonds of earth

And danced the skies on laughter-silvered wings;

Sunward I've climbed and joined the tumbling mirth

Of sun-split clouds – and done a hundred things

You have not dreamed of: wheeled and soared and swung

High in the sun-lit silence. Hovering there

I've chased the shouting wind along, and flung

My eager craft through footless halls of air;

Up, up the long, delirious, burning blue

I've topped the wind-swept heights with easy grace,

Where never lark nor even eagle flew;

And while, with silent lifting mind I've trod

The high untrespassed sanctity of space,

Put out my hand, and touched the face of God.

John Gillespie Magee

1922–41, b. Shanghai

In 1940, Magee enlisted into the Royal Canadian Airforce to fight Hitler's Germany. He was posted to England in June of the following year as Pilot Officer. On 3 September, he flew a high altitude test in a Spitfire V and was inspired to write this poem, which he copied out in a letter to his parents. Three months later, the 19 year-old was killed when his plane collided with another English aircraft in thick cloud.

WAR AND HEROISM

from The Charge of the Light Brigade

I   Half a league, half a league,
       Half a league onward,
    All in the valley of Death
       Rode the six hundred.
    'Forward, the Light Brigade!
    Charge for the guns!' he said;
    Into the valley of Death
       Rode the six hundred.

II   'Forward, the Light Brigade!'
    Was there a man dismay'd?
    Not tho' the soldier knew
       Some one had blunder'd:
    Their's not to make reply,
    Their's not to reason why,
    Their's but to do and die:
    Into the valley of Death
       Rode the six hundred.

III Cannon to right of them,
    Cannon to left of them,
    Cannon in front of them
       Volley'd and thunder'd;
    Stormed at with shot and
    shell,
    Boldly they rode and well,
    Into the jaws of Death,
    Into the mouth of Hell
    Rode the six hundred.

Alfred, Lord Tennyson
1809–92, b. England

During the Crimean War, there was a charge at Balaclava on 25 October 1854 when 247 out of 637 soldiers were killed or wounded – due to a misunderstood order. This poem appeared in the Examiner only weeks later. The line 'Someone had blundered', suggested by a phrase in a report in The Times, was omitted when it was published in 1855 in Maud, and Other Poems, but was later reinstated.

79

II

He did not come in the dawning; he did not come at noon;
And out o' the tawny sunset, before the rise o' the moon,
When the road was a gipsy's ribbon, looping the purple moor,
A red-coat troop came marching –
  Marching – marching –
King George's men came marching, up to the old inn-door.

They said no word to the landlord, they drank his ale instead,
But they gagged his daughter and bound her to the foot of her narrow bed;
Two of them knelt at her casement, with muskets at their side!
There was death at every window:
  And hell at one dark window;
For Bess could see, through her casement, the road that he would ride.
They had tied her up to attention, with many a sniggering jest;
They had bound a musket beside her, with the barrel beneath her breast!
'Now keep good watch!' and they kissed her.
  She heard the dead man say –
Look for me by moonlight;
  Watch for me by moonlight;
I'll come to thee by moonlight, though hell should bar the way!

She twisted her hands behind her; but all the knots held good!
She writhed her hands till her fingers were wet with sweat or blood!
They stretched and strained in the darkness, and the hours crawled by like years,
Till, now, on the stroke of midnight,
    Cold, on the stroke of midnight,
The tip of one finger touched it! The trigger at least was hers!

The tip of one finger touched it; she strove no more for the rest!
Up, she stood to attention, with the barrel beneath her breast,
She would not risk their hearing; she would not strive again;
For the road lay bare in the moonlight:
    Blank and bare in the moonlight:
And the blood of her veins in the moonlight throbbed to her love's refrain.

Tlot-tlot; tloy-tlot! Had they heard it? The horse-hooves ringing clear;
Tlot-tlot, tlot-tlot, in the distance? Were they deaf that they did not hear?
Down the ribbon of moonlight, over the brow of the hill,
The highwayman came riding,
    Riding, riding!
The red-coats looked to their priming! She stood up, straight and still!
Tlot-tlot, in the frosty silence! *tlot-tlot*, in the echoing night!

Nearer he came and nearer! Her face was like a light!
Her eyes grew wide for a moment; she drew one last deep breath,
Then her finger moved in the moonlight,
 Her musket shattered the moonlight,
Shattered her breast in the moonlight and warned him – with her death.

He turned; he spurred to the westward; he did not know who stood
Bowed, with her head o'er the musket, drenched with her own red blood!
Not till the dawn he heard it, and slowly blanched to hear
 How Bess, the landlord's daughter,
  The landlord's black-eyed daughter,
Had watched for her love in the moonlight, and died in the darkness there.

Back, he spurred like a madman, shrieking a curse to the sky,
With the white road smoking behind him and his rapier brandished high!
Blood-red were his spurs i' the golden noon; wine-red was his velvet coat;
When they shot him down on the highway,
 Down like a dog on the highway,
And he lay in his blood on the highway, with the bunch of lace at his throat.

And still of a winter's night, they say, when the wind is in the trees,
When the moon is a ghostly galleon tossed upon cloudy seas,
When the road is a ribbon of moonlight over the purple moor,
A highwayman comes riding –
    Riding – riding –
A highwayman comes riding, up to the old inn-door.

Over the cobbles he clatters and clangs in the dark inn-yard
And he taps with his whip on the shutters, but all is locked and barred;
He whistles a tune to the window, and who should be waiting there
But the landlord's black-eyed daughter,
    Bess, the landlord's daughter,
Plaiting a dark red love-knot into her long black hair.

Alfred Noyes

1880–1959, b. England

A *poet, playwright, novelist, and anthologist, Alfred Noyes also taught English literature at Princeton University in the United States between 1914–1923. He violently disagreed with the Modernist movement's experimentalism and focus on the subconscious, and his own work follows the narrative, descriptive tradition of the Victorians and Edwardians. The Highwayman is loved by readers of all ages the world over, and has inspired several folk songs.*

The Star-Spangled Banner

O say, can you see, by the dawn's early light,
    What so proudly we hailed at the twilights' last gleaming –
Whose broad stripes and bright stars, through the clouds of the fight,
    O'er the ramparts we watched were so gallantly streaming!
And the rocket's red glare, the bombs bursting in air,
Gave proof through the night that our flag was still there;
O! say, does that star-spangled banner yet wave
O'er the land of the free, and the home of the brave?

On that shore dimly seen through the mists of the deep,
    Where the foe's haughty host in dread silence reposes,
What is that which the breeze, o'er the towering steep,
    As it fitfully flows, now conceals, now discloses?
Now it catches the gleam of the morning's first beam,
In full glory reflected now shines on the stream;
Tis the star-spangled banner; O long may it wave
O'er the land of the free, and the home of the brave!

And where is that band who so vauntingly swore
    That the havoc of war and the battles' confusion
A home and a country should leave us no more?
    Their blood has washed out their foul footsteps' pollution.
No refuge could save the hireling and slave
From the terror of flight, or the gloom of the grave;
And the star-spangled banner in triumph doth wave
O'er the land of the free, and the home of the brave.

O! thus be it ever, when freemen shall stand
　　　Between their loved homes and the war's desolation!
Blest with victory and peace, may the heav'n-rescued land
　　　Praise the power that hath made and preserved us a nation.
Then conquer we must, when our cause it is just,
And this be our motto – 'In God is our trust':
And the star-spangled banner in triumph shall wave
O'er the land of the free, and the home of the brave.

Francis Scott Key

1779–1843, b. USA

It was the sight of the American flag flying over Fort McHenry in Baltimore Harbour, during the 1812 war with Britain, that inspired lawyer and poet Francis Scott Key to write this poem. Written on the back of a letter, the poem is set to the tune of an English drinking song. It became the national anthem of the United States on March 3, 1931. A copy Key made of his original poem is in the Library of Congress.

Sir Patrick Spence

The king sits in Dumferling toune,
 Drinking the blude-reid wine:
'O whar will I get a guid sailor,
 To sail this schip of mine?'

Up and spak an eldern knicht,
 Sat at the king's richt kne:
'Sir Patrick Spence is the best sailor,
 That sails upon the se.'

The king has written a braid letter,
 And signed it wi' his hand;
And sent it to Sir Patrick Spence,
 Was walking on the sand.

The first line that Sir Patrick red,
 A loud lauch lauched he:
The next line that Sir Patrick red,
 The teir blinded his e'e.

'O wha is this has don this deid,
 This ill deid don to me:
To send me out this time o' the yeir,
 To sail upon the se?

'Mak haste, mak haste, my mirry men all,
 Our guid schip sails the morne.'
'O say na sae, my master deir,
 For I feir a deadlie storme.

'Late, late yestreen I saw the new moone
 Wi' the auld moone in hir arme;
And I feir, I feir, my deir master,
 That we will com to harme.'

from The Iliad

Now shield with shield, with helmet helmet closed,
To armour armour, lance to lance opposed,
Host against host with shadowy squadrons drew,
The sounding darts in iron tempests flew,
Victors and vanquished joined promiscuous cries,
And shrilling shouts and dying groans arise;
With streaming blood the slippery fields are dyed,
And slaughtered heroes swell the dreadful tide.

　　As torrents roll, increased by numerous rills,
With rage impetuous down their echoing ills,
Rush to the vales, and poured along the plain,
Roar through a thousand channels to the main;
The distant shepherd trembling hears the sound:
So mix both hosts, and so their cries rebound.

Homer
translated by Alexander Pope
1688–1744, b. England

Homer was more important to the Classical world than Shakespeare is to us today. His poems provided the basis of Ancient Greek and Roman education. Set in the imaginary heroic past of the Trojan war, The Iliad centres on the bitter quarrel between Agamemmon and Achilles, the greatest of the Greek warriors. Its over 15,000 lines starkly depict the glory, and brutality, of war. This extract describes the recommencing of battle between the two sides after a truce has been breached.

Anthem for Doomed Youth

What passing-bells for these who die as cattle?
    Only the monstrous anger of the guns.
    Only the stuttering rifles' rapid rattle
Can patter out their hasty orisons.
No mockeries now for them; no prayers nor bells.
    Nor any voice of mourning save the choirs, –
The shrill, demented choirs of wailing shells;
    And bugles calling for them from sad shires.

What candles may be held to speed them all?
    Not in the hands of boys, but in their eyes
Shall shine the holy glimmers of good-byes.
    The pallor of girls' brows shall be their pall;
Their flowers the tenderness of patient minds,
And each slow dusk a drawing down of blinds.

Wilfred Owen
1893–1918, b. England

The son of a railway-worker, Wilfred Owen read widely and began writing poetry at an early age. He taught English in Bordeaux in 1913, and returned there in 1915 to join the army. After enduring concussion and trench-fever on the Somme, Owen was sent to hospital in Edinburgh. There he met and was encouraged in his writing by Siegfried Sassoon (who was suffering from shell-shock). Owen returned to France in 1918, won the Military Cross, and was killed a week before the Armistice.

from Beowulf

After these words the Weather-Geat prince
dived into the Mere – he did not care
to wait for an answer – and the waves closed over
the daring man. It was a day's space almost
before he could glimpse ground at the bottom.

The grim and greedy guardian of the flood,
keeping her hungry hundred-season watch,
discovered at once that one from above,
a human, had sounded the home of the monsters.
She felt for the man and fastened upon him
her terrible hooks; but no harm came thereby
to the hale body within – the harness so ringed him
that she could not drive her dire fingers
through the mesh of the mail-shirt masking his limbs.

Dulce Et Decorum Est

Bent double, like old beggars under sacks,
Knock-kneed, coughing like hags, we cursed through sludge,
Till on the haunting flares we turned our backs
And towards our distant rest began to trudge.
Men marched asleep. Many had lost their boots
But limped on, blood-shod. All went lame; all blind;
Drunk with fatigue; deaf even to the hoots
Of tired, outstripped Five-Nines that dropped behind.

Gas! Gas! Quick, boys! – An ecstasy of fumbling,
Fitting the clumsy helmets just in time;
But someone still was yelling out and stumbling
And flound'ring like a man in fire or lime . . .
Dim, through the misty panes and thick green light,
As under a green sea, I saw him drowning.

In all my dreams, before my helpless sight,
He plunges at me, guttering, choking, drowning.

If in some smothering dreams you too could pace
Behind the wagon that we flung him in,
And watch the white eyes writhing in his face,
His hanging face, like a devil's sick of sin;
If you could hear, at every jolt, the blood
Come gargling from the froth-corrupted lungs,
Obscene as cancer, bitter as the cud
Of vile, incurable sores on innocent tongues, –
My friend, you would not tell with such high zest
To children ardent for some desperate glory,
The old Lie: Dulce et decorum est
Pro patria mori.

Wilfred Owen
1893–1918, b. England

Owen is now considered to be the foremost poet of World War I. However, only five of his poems were published during his lifetime and they achieved no success – like Siegfried Sassoon's war poetry. The public were captivated by Rupert Brooke, whose often wistful poems speak of glory and heroism and the enduring qualities of love. The work of both Sassoon and Owen tells bleakly of the miserable reality of the trenches and expresses contempt for war.

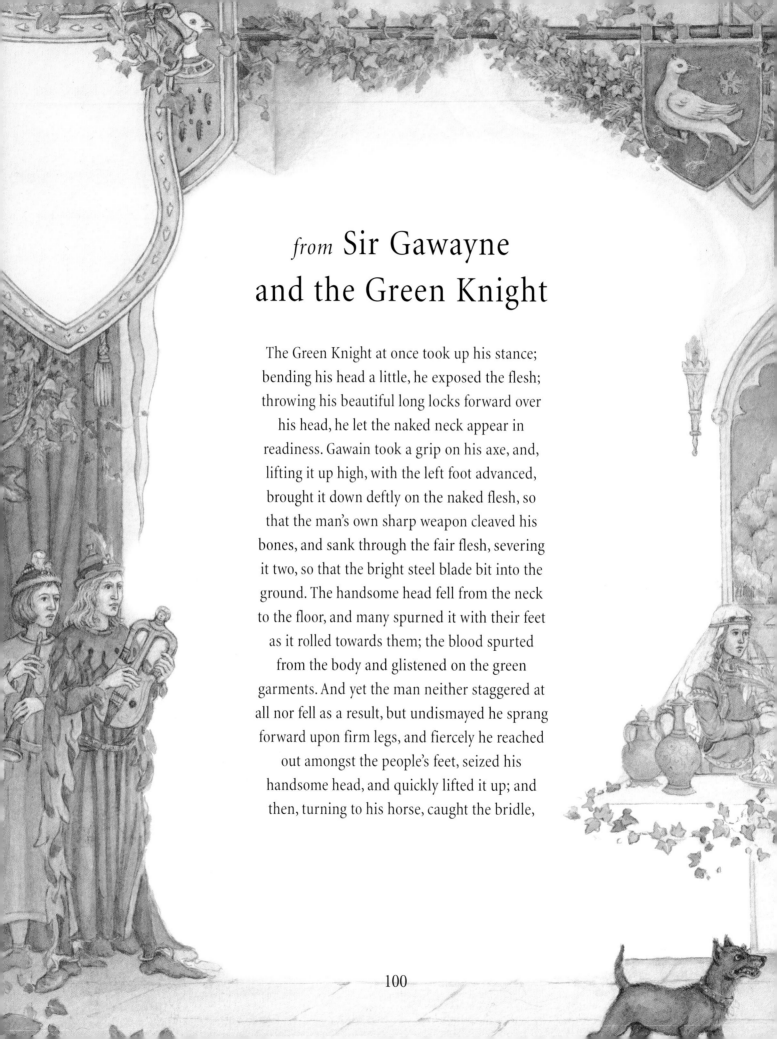

from Sir Gawayne and the Green Knight

The Green Knight at once took up his stance; bending his head a little, he exposed the flesh; throwing his beautiful long locks forward over his head, he let the naked neck appear in readiness. Gawain took a grip on his axe, and, lifting it up high, with the left foot advanced, brought it down deftly on the naked flesh, so that the man's own sharp weapon cleaved his bones, and sank through the fair flesh, severing it two, so that the bright steel blade bit into the ground. The handsome head fell from the neck to the floor, and many spurned it with their feet as it rolled towards them; the blood spurted from the body and glistened on the green garments. And yet the man neither staggered at all nor fell as a result, but undismayed he sprang forward upon firm legs, and fiercely he reached out amongst the people's feet, seized his handsome head, and quickly lifted it up; and then, turning to his horse, caught the bridle,

stepped into the stirrup and vaulted up,
holding his head by the hair in his hand, and the
knight seated himself in his saddle as calmly as
if he had suffered no mishap, though he sat there
headless now. He twisted his trunk around, that
gruesome bleeding corpse; many were afraid of
him by the time he had had his say.

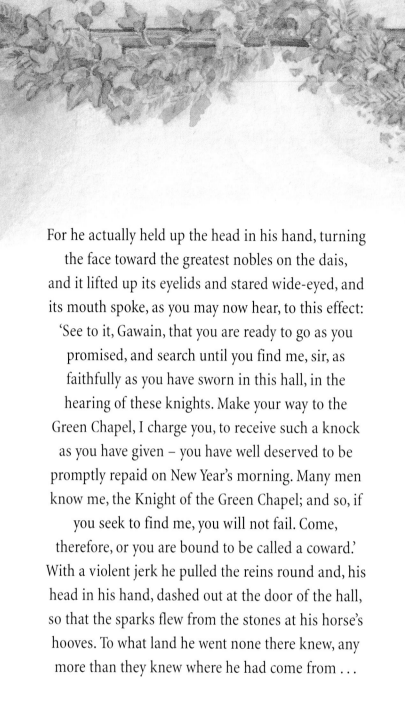

For he actually held up the head in his hand, turning
the face toward the greatest nobles on the dais,
and it lifted up its eyelids and stared wide-eyed, and
its mouth spoke, as you may now hear, to this effect:
'See to it, Gawain, that you are ready to go as you
promised, and search until you find me, sir, as
faithfully as you have sworn in this hall, in the
hearing of these knights. Make your way to the
Green Chapel, I charge you, to receive such a knock
as you have given – you have well deserved to be
promptly repaid on New Year's morning. Many men
know me, the Knight of the Green Chapel; and so, if
you seek to find me, you will not fail. Come,
therefore, or you are bound to be called a coward.'
With a violent jerk he pulled the reins round and, his
head in his hand, dashed out at the door of the hall,
so that the sparks flew from the stones at his horse's
hooves. To what land he went none there knew, any
more than they knew where he had come from . . .

Anon *circa 1375*

translated by WRJ Barron

This famous medieval poem combines
English 'green man' folklore with
Arthurian legend. A huge green warrior
bursts into King Arthur's New Year Feast.
He challenges a knight to cut off his head –
on condition that he can return the blow in
a year's time. Sir Gawain courageously
accepts, but is horrified to find that the
Green Knight simply picks up his head and
rides away, laughing. Twelve months later,
brave Gawain has to set off to honour the
bargain . . .

from Morte d'Arthur

So all day long the noise of battle rolled
Among the mountains by the winter sea;
Until King Arthur's table, man by man,
Had fallen in Lyonnesse about their Lord,
King Arthur. Then, because his wound was deep,
The bold Sir Bedivere uplifted him,
Sir Bedivere, the last of all his knights,
And bore him to a chapel nigh the field,
A broken chancel with a broken cross,
That stood on a dark strait of barren land.
On one side lay the Ocean, and on one
Lay a great water, and the moon was full.

Then spake King Arthur to Sir Bedivere:
'...I perish by this perople which I made, –
Though Merlin sware that I should come again
To rule once more – but let what will be, be,
I am so deeply smitten through the helm
That without help I cannot last till morn.
Thou therefore take my brand Excalibur,
Which was my pride: for thou rememberest how
In those old days, one summer noon, an arm
Rose up from out of the bosom of the lake,
Clothed in white samite, mystic, wonderful,
Holding the sword – and how I rowed across
And took it, and have worn it, like a king:
And, wheresoever I am sung or told
In aftertime, this also shall be known:
But now delay not: take Excalibur,
And fling him far into the middle mere:
Watch what thou seest, and lightly bring me word.'

...Then quickly rose Sir Bedivere, and ran,
And, leaping down the ridges lightly, plunged
Among the bulrush-beds, and clutched the sword,
And strongly wheeled and threw it. The great brand
Made lightnings in the splendour of the moon,
And flashing round and round, and whirled in an arch,
Shot like a streamer of the northern morn,
Seen where the moving isles of winter shock
By night, with noises of the northern sea.
So flashed and fell the brand Excalibur:
But ere he dipt the surface, rose an arm
Clothed in white samite, mystic, wonderful,
And caught him by the hilt, and brandished him
Three times, and drew him under in the mere.

Alfred, Lord Tennyson
1809–92, b. England

Tennyson began this poem in 1833, soon after the death of his best friend, Arthur Hallam. As a source, he used Malory's huge collection of Arthurian legends Le Morte D'Arthur (finished 1470). The poem tells of the king's last moments, after battling the usurping Mordred. In 1869, Tennyson added 169 lines to the start and 29 lines at the end, and incorporated the poem into his 12 book cycle of Arthurian ballads, the Idylls of the King.

LOVE

from The Bible
I Corinthians 13, 1-13

If I speak in the tongues of men and of angels, but have not love, I am a noisy gong or a clanging cymbal. And if I have prophetic powers, and understand all mysteries and all knowledge, and if I have all faith, so as to remove mountains, but have not love, I am nothing. If I give away all I have, and if I deliver my body to be burned, but have not love, I gain nothing.

Love is patient and kind; love is not jealous or boastful; it is not arrogant or rude. Love does not insist on its own way; it is not irritable or resentful; it does not rejoice at wrong, but rejoices in the right. Love bears all things, believes all things, hopes all things, endures all things.

Love never ends; as for prophecies, they will pass away; as for tongues, they will cease; as for knowledge, it will pass away. For our knowledge is imperfect and our prophecy is imperfect; but when the perfect comes, the imperfect will pass away. When I was a child, I spoke like a child, I thought like a child, I reasoned like a child; when I became a man, I gave up childish ways. For now we see in a mirror dimly, but then face to face. Now I know in part; then I shall understand fully, even as I have been fully understood. So faith, hope, love abide, these three; but the greatest of these is love.

St Paul

circa 50 AD

So
faith, hope,
love
abide,
these three;
but the
greatest of these is
love

After the death of Jesus, his apostles travelled around the Mediterranean and Asia Minor, establishing communities of disciples. Letters were a vital way of keeping in touch with these early churches, who needed constant teaching and support.

More Bible letters are attributed to Paul than to any other apostle, and these inspiring lines, now often read aloud at weddings and on other significant occasions, are from Paul's first letter to the Corinthians.

A Red, Red Rose

My love is like a red, red rose
    That's newly sprung in June:
My love is like the melody
    That's sweetly played in tune.

As fair art thou, my bonnie lass,
    So deep in love am I:
And I will love thee still, my dear,
    Till a' the seas gang dry.

Till a' the seas gang dry, my dear,
    And the rocks melt wi' the sun:
And I will love thee still, my dear,
    While the sands o' life shall run.

And fare thee weel, my only love,
    And fare thee weel a while!
And I will come again, my love,
    Thou' it were ten thousand mile.

Robert Burns

1759–96, b. Scotland

A struggling farmer, Burns' *Poems, Chiefly in the Scottish Dialect (1786)* made him an overnight success, acclaimed by Edinburgh literary circles as a 'Heaven-taught ploughman'. The lyric A Red, Red Rose *was one of 200 Scottish songs he wrote* and collected for *The Scots Musical Museum. Still honoured as Scotland's finest poet, Scots all over the world remember Burns's birthday, 25 January, in a celebration, often marked by haggis and poetry, called Burns Night.*

Sonnet 116

Let me not to the marriage of true minds
Admit impediments. Love is not love
Which alters when it alteration finds,
Or bends with the remover to remove:
O, no, it is an ever-fixèd mark,
That looks on tempests and is never shaken;
It is the star to every wandering bark,
Whose worth's unknown, although his height be taken.
Love's not Time's fool, though rosy lips and cheeks
Within his bending sickle's compass come;
Love alters not with his brief hours and weeks,
But bears it out even to the edge of doom.
      If this be error and upon my proved,
      I never writ, nor no man ever loved.

William Shakespeare
1564–1616, b. England

The writing of sonnets (14 line poems which follow a set rhyme scheme) became extremely fashionable in 16th century Europe. The witty love poems were written in series called 'cycles', usually addressing a lady and following the thread of a story. Shakespeare's sonnets are unique for their profound thoughts, and also in that the person addressed is sometimes not a woman, but a young man.

She Walks in Beauty

She walks in beauty, like the night
    Of cloudless climes and starry skies;
And all that's best of dark and bright
    Meet in her aspect and her eyes:
Thus mellow'd to that tender light
    Which heaven to gaudy day denies.

One shade the more, one ray the less,
    Had half impair'd the nameless grace
Which waves in every raven tress,
    Or softly lightens o'er her face;
Where thoughts serenely sweet express
    How pure, how dear their dwelling-place.

And on that cheek, and o'er that brow,
    So soft, so calm, yet eloquent,
The smiles that win, the tints that glow,
    But tell of days in goodness spent,
A mind at peace with all below,
    A heart whose love is innocent!

Lord Byron
1788–1824, b. England

Byron's poetry was frequently attacked by critics as immoral, yet was immensely popular. Byron himself was just as controversial. Irresistibly handsome, he had homosexual experiences as well as countless love affairs with women. Cast out of English society after his half-sister gave birth to their daughter, he settled in Italy, where he engaged in revolutionary activity. After financing, training and leading the Greeks in rebellion against the Turks, Byron died at only 36 years old.

He Wishes for the Cloths of Heaven

Had I the heavens' embroidered cloths,
Enwrought with golden and silver light,
The blue and the dim and the dark cloths
Of night and light and the half-light,
I would spread the cloths under your feet:
But I, being poor, have only my dreams;
I have spread my dreams under your feet;
Tread softly because you tread on my dreams.

W B Yeats

1865–1939, b. Eire

Poet and playwright William Butler Yeats originally trained to be an artist like his father and brother. A great admirer of Blake (whose collected poems he edited), he developed a life-long interest in mystic religion and the supernatural. As well as Irish traditional themes, his unrequited love for Irish revolutionary Maude Gonne inspired much of his early poetry, including the collection The Wind Among the Reeds (1899) from which this particular poem comes.

Sonnet 18

Shall I compare thee to a summer's day?
Thou art more lovely and more temperate:
Rough winds do shake the darling buds of May,
And summer's lease hath all too short a date;
Sometime too hot the eye of heaven shines,
And often is his gold complexion dimm'd,
And every fair from fair sometime declines,
By chance or nature's changing course untrimm'd:
But thy eternal summer shall not fade,
Nor lose possession of that fair thou ow'st,
Nor shall Death brag thou wand'rest in his shade,
When in eternal lines to time thou grow'st.
    So long as men can breathe or eyes can see,
    So long lives this, and this gives life to thee.

William Shakespeare
1564–1616, b. England

Shakespeare's cycle of 154 sonnets was published in 1609, and probably written between 1592–96. The first 126 seem addressed to a male friend, often urging him to marry and have children. The following 26 involve the seduction of the friend by a mysterious 'dark lady'. The two final sonnets are translations of Greek wit. Many scholars have failed to identify real people with the friend and the 'dark lady'.

So, we'll go
no more a-roving

So, we'll go no more a-roving
    So late into the night,
Though the heart be still as loving,
    And the moon be still as bright.

For the sword outwears its sheath,
    And the soul wears out the breast,
And the heart must pause to breathe,
    And love itself have rest.

Though the night was made for loving,
    And the day returns too soon,
Yet we'll go no more a-roving
    By the light of the moon.

Lord Byron

1788–1824, b. England

This poem was written in 1817, when Byron was enjoying a riotous and exhausting social life in Venice. Byron wrote the phrase 'so we'll go no more a-roving' in a letter to Thomas Moore, in which he admitted that his hedonistic lifestyle was wearing him out – '. . . yet I find "the sword wearing out the scabbard", though I have but just turned the corner of 29.'

On the Ning Nang Nong

On the Ning Nang Nong
Where the Cows go Bong!
And the Monkeys all say Boo!
There's a Nong Nang Ning
Where the trees go Ping!
And the tea pots Jibber Jabber Joo.
On the Nong Ning Nang
All the mice go Clang!
And you just can't catch 'em when they do!
So it's Ning Nang Nong!
Cows go Bong!
Nong Nang Ning!
Trees go Ping!
Nong Ning Nang!
The mice go Clang!
What a noisy place to belong,
Is the Ning Nang Ning Nang Nong!!

Spike Milligan

b. 1918, India

Spike Milligan is one of Britain's best-loved comedians. He was a star of radio's **The Goon Show,** famous from the 1950s, and has since performed much on TV. A great writer of nonsense verse following the tradition of Edward Lear, his humorous books for children have an irresistible whackiness and include Silly Verse for Kids (1959) and Unspun Socks from a Chicken's Laundry (1981).

Who's Who

I used to think nurses
Were women,
I used to think police
Were men,
I used to think poets
Were boring,
Until I became one of them.

Benjamin Zephaniah
b. 1958, England

Benjamin Zephaniah had his childhood in Jamaica. He writes poetry that is meant to be performed aloud, rather than read to oneself. This type of poetry was a growing trend throughout the 20th century, and the literary culture of 'dub', as it is known, has its roots in the street culture of 'rap'. Zephaniah is part of an exceptional black performance poetry scene that includes: Linton Kwesi Johnson, John Agard, Grace Nichols, Lemn Sissay, and Valerie Bloom.

Some one

Some one came knocking
    At my wee, small door;
Some one came knocking,
    I'm sure – sure – sure;
I listened, I opened,
    I looked to left and right,
But nought there was a-stirring
    In the still dark night;
Only the busy beetle
    Tap-tapping in the wall,
Only from the forest
    The screech-owl's call,
Only the cricket whistling
    While the dewdrops fall,
So I know not who came knocking,
    At all, at all, at all.

Walter de la Mare

1873–1956, b. England

Walter de la Mare's first book, Songs of Childhood (1902), attracted little attention. Undismayed, he continued writing for both adults and children, and went on to publish many poetry collections, novels and short stories to high acclaim. The widespread popularity of his poems has endured over generations due to his unaffected style. His ashes are buried in St Paul's Cathedral.

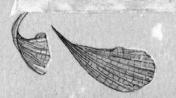

from

The Fairies

Up the airy mountain
Down the rushy glen,
We daren't go a-hunting
For fear of little men;
Wee folk, good folk,
Trooping all together;
Green jacket, red cap,
And white owl's feather!

William Allingham

1824–89, b. Eire

Customs Officer William Allingham composed several collections and anthologies of verse for children, some with illustrations by Rossetti, Millais, Kate Greenaway, and his wife, Helen Paterson. The Fairies (written in 1840) was published in his Poems (1850). It is based on a traditional song that was adapted in Scotland to the Jacobite cause: 'Tis up the rocky mountain and down the mossy glen, We darena gang a milking for Charlie and his men . . . '

133

Then into the chamber turning, all my soul within me burning.
Soon again I heard a tapping somewhat louder than before.
'Surely,' said I, 'surely that is something at my window lattice;
Let me see, then, what thereat is, and this mystery explore –
Let my heart be still a moment, and this mystery explore; –
　　　'Tis the wind and nothing more.'

Open here I flung the shutter, when, with many a flirt and flutter,
In there stepped a stately Raven of the saintly days of yore.
Not the least obeisance made he; not an instant stopped or stayed he;
But, with mien of lord or lady, perched above my chamber door –
Perched upon a bust of Pallas just above my chamber door –
　　　Perched, and sat, and nothing more.

Then this ebony bird beguiling my sad fancy into smiling,
By the grave and stern decorum of the countenance it wore,
'Though thy crest be shorn and shaven, thou,' I said, 'art sure no craven,
Ghastly grim and ancient Raven wandering from the Nightly shore –
Tell me what thy Lordly name is on the Night's Plutonian shore!'
Quoth the Raven, 'Nevermore.'

*　　*　　*

But the Raven, sitting lonely on that placid bust, spoke only
That one word, as if his soul in that one word he did outpour.
Nothing further then he uttered; not a feather then he fluttered –
Till I scarcely more than muttered, 'Other friends have flown before –
On the morrow *he* will leave me, as my Hopes have flown before.'
　　　Then the bird said, 'Nevermore.'

*   *   *

'Prophet!' said I, 'thing of evil – prophet still, if bird or devil!
By that Heaven that bends above us – by that God we both adore –
Tell this soul with sorrow laden if, within the distant Aidenn,
It shall clasp a sainted maiden whom the angels name Lenore –
Clasp a rare and radiant maiden whom the angels name Lenore.'
    Quoth the Raven, 'Nevermore.'

'Be that word our sign of parting, bird or fiend!' I shrieked, upstarting –
'Get thee back into the tempest and the Night's Plutonian shore!
Leave no black plume as a token of that lie thy soul hath spoken!
Leave my loneliness unbroken! – quit the bust above my door!'
Take thy beak from out my heart, and take thy form from off my door!'
    Quoth the Raven, 'Nevermore.'

And the Raven, never flitting, still is sitting – still is sitting
On the pallid bust of Pallas just above my chamber door;
And his eyes have all the seeming of a Demon's that is dreaming,
And the lamp-light o'er him streaming throws his shadow on the floor;
And my soul from out that shadow that lies floating on the floor
    Shall be lifted – nevermore!

Edgar Allen Poe

1809–49, b. USA

Journalist Edgar Allen Poe was a master of macabre mystery stories such as The Pit and the Pendulum. However, he began his writing career as a poet, publishing his first volume of verse in 1827 anonymously and at his own expense. The Raven first appeared in 1845 in a New York newspaper, and The Raven and other Poems *(1845)* finally brought him fame – although not fortune. He struggled with poverty, nervous instability and alcoholism and died at the age of 40.

Jabberwocky

1. 'Twas brillig, and the slithy toves
   Did gyre and gimble in the wabe;
   All mimsy were the borogoves,
   And the mome raths outgrabe.

2. 'Beware the Jabberwock, my son!
   The jaws that bite, the claws that catch!
   Beware the Jubjub bird, and shun
   The frumious Bandersnatch!'

3. He took his vorpal sword in hand;
   Long time the manxome foe he sought –
   So rested he by the Tumtum tree,
   And stood awhile in thought.

4. And, as in uffish thought he stood,
   The Jabberwock, with eyes of flame,
   Came whiffling through the tulgey wood,
   And burbled as it came!

5. One, two! One two! And through and through
   The vorpal blade went snicker-snack!
   He left it dead, and with its head
   He went galumphing back.

6. 'And hast thou slain the Jabberwock?
   Come to my arms, my beamish boy!
   O frabjous day! Callooh! Callay!'
   He chortled in his joy.

7. 'Twas brillig, and the slithy toves
   Did gyre and gimble in the wabe:
   All mimsy were the borogoves,
   And the mome raths outgrabe.

Lewis Carroll
1832–98, b. England

*L*ewis Carroll was the pen-name of Charles Lutwidge Dodgson. While a maths lecturer at Christ Church, Oxford, he wrote the classic novels Alice's Adventures in Wonderland (1865) and Through the Looking-Glass *and* What Alice Found There (1871). His poetry includes Phantasmagoria and other poems (1869) *and* The Hunting of the Snark (1876). Most writing for children at the time had a moral message, and Carroll's fantastical novels and comic verse were immensely popular.

from The Ballad of Reading Gaol

1. There is no chapel on the day
   On which they hang a man:
   The Chaplain's heart is far too sick,
   Or his face is far too wan,
   Or there is that written in his eyes
   Which none should look upon.

2. So they kept us close till night on noon,
   And then they rang the bell,
   And the Warders with their jingling keys
   Opened each listening cell,
   And down the iron stair we tramped,
   Each from his separate Hell.

3. Out into God's sweet air we went,
   But not in wonted way,
   For this man's face was white with fear,
   And that man's face was gray,
   And I never saw sad men who looked
   So wistfully at the day.

4. I never saw sad men who looked
   With such a wistful eye
   Upon that little tent of blue
   We prisoners call the sky,
   And at every careless cloud that passed
   In happy freedom by.

5. The Warders strutted up and down,
   And kept their herd of brutes,
   Their uniforms were spick and span,
   And they wore their Sunday suits,
   But we knew the work they had been at,
   By the quicklime on their boots.

6. For where a grave had opened wide,
   There was no grave at all:
   Only a stretch of mud and sand
   By the hideous prison-wall,
   And a little heaping of burning lime,
   That the man should have his pall.

Dreams

Here we are all, by day; by night we're hurled
By dreams, each one, into a several world.

Robert Herrick

1591–1674, b. England

Robert Herrick was ordained as a vicar in 1623 at the age of 32, when he was already a well-known poet. Six years later, he went to be a vicar in Dean Prior, a village on the edge of Dartmoor, where he lived for the rest of his life. He wrote over a thousand short poems altogether, often on country customs and beliefs, his household – including his cat and dog (a spaniel named Tracy) – and death and transience. Most were published in *Hesperides* (1648).

'The night is darkening round me'

The night is darkening round me,
The wild winds coldly blow;
But a tyrant spell has bound me
And I cannot, cannot go.

The giant trees are bending
Their bare boughs weighed with snow,
The storm is fast descending
And yet I cannot go.

Clouds beyond clouds above me,
Wastes beyond wastes below;
But nothing drear can move me;
I will not, cannot go.

Emily Brontë

1818–1848, b. England

Emily Brontë loved her isolated home on the bleak Yorkshire moors with a passion. Her sisters, Charlotte and Anne, convinced Emily to have a selection of their poems published pseudonymously in 1846 – only two copies were sold. The following year, Emily's novel Wuthering Heights, *was published with scant recognition, and in 1848 she died of tuberculosis. Today, Emily Brontë ranks among the greatest English poets and* Wuthering Heights *is considered a masterpiece.*

The Way through the Woods

They shut the road through the woods
Seventy years ago.
Weather and rain have undone it again,
And now you would never know
There was once a road through the woods
Before they planted the trees.
It is underneath the coppice and heath,
And the thin anemones.
Only the keeper sees
That, where the ring-dove broods,
And the badgers roll at ease,
There was once a road through the woods.

Yet, if you enter the woods
Of a summer evening late,
When the night-air cools on the trout-ringed pools
Where the otter whistles his mate,
(They fear not men in the woods,
Because they see so few.)
You will hear the beat of a horses's feet,
And the swish of a skirt in the dew,
Steadily cantering through
The misty solitudes,
As though they perfectly knew
The old lost road through the woods . . .
But there is no road through the woods.

Rudyard Kipling

1865–1936, b. India

Born in India but educated in England, Kipling returned there in 1881 to work as a journalist. Many of his early poems and stories were originally published in newspapers or for the Indian Railway Library. His best-loved works include **The** **Jungle Book** *(1894),* **Kim** *(1901) and* **Just So** **Stories** *(1902). Never the Poet Laureate many thought he should have been, he refused many honours. However, in 1907 he was the first English writer to receive the Nobel Prize.*

CHRISTMAS

The Night Before Christmas

'Twas the night before Christmas, when all through the house
Not a creature was stirring, not even a mouse;
The stockings were hung by the chimney with care,
In hopes that St Nicholas soon would be there;
The children were nestled all snug in their beds,
While visions of sugar plums danced in their heads;
And mamma in her 'kerchief, and I in my cap,
Had just settled our brains for a long winter's nap,
When out on the lawn there arose such a clatter,
I sprang from the bed to see what was the matter.
Away to the window I flew like a flash,
Tore open the shutters and threw up the sash.

The moon on the breast of the new-fallen snow
Gave the lustre of midday to objects below,
When, what to my wondering eyes should appear,
But a miniature sleigh, and eight tiny reindeer,
With a little old driver, so lively and quick,
I knew in a moment it must be St Nick.
More rapid than eagles his coursers they came,
And he whistled, and shouted, and called them by name:
'Now, Dasher! now, Dancer! now, Prancer and Vixen!
On, Comet! on, Cupid! on, Donder and Blitzen!
To the top of the porch! to the top of the wall!
Now dash away! dash away! dash away all!'
As dry leaves that before the wild hurricane fly,
When they meet with an obstacle, mount to the sky,
So up to the house-top the coursers they flew,
With the sleigh full of toys, and St Nicholas too.

Balloons

Since Christmas they have lived with us,
Guileless and clear,
Oval soul-animals,
Taking up half the space,
Moving and rubbing on the silk

Invisible air drifts,
Giving a shriek and pop
When attacked, then scooting to rest, barely trembling.
Yellow cathead, blue fish –
Such queer moons we live with

Instead of dead furniture!
Straw mats, white walls
And these travelling
Globes of thin air, red, green,
Delighting

The heart like wishes or free
Peacocks blessing
Old ground with a feather
Beaten in starry metals.
Your small

Brother is making
His balloons squeak like a cat.
Seeming to see
A funny pink world he might eat on the other side of it,
He bites,

Then sits
Back, fat jug
Contemplating a world clear as water.
A red
Shred in his little fist

Sylvia Plath

1932–63, b. USA

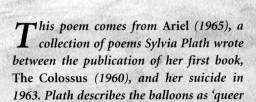

This poem comes from Ariel (1965), a collection of poems Sylvia Plath wrote between the publication of her first book, The Colossus (1960), and her suicide in 1963. Plath describes the balloons as 'queer moons' – the moon was one of many recurring themes in her work, along with glass, blood, hospitals and death. The 'brother' in the poem is Plath's second child with Ted Hughes, Nicholas, born in 1962.

LIFE AND DEATH

'Death be not proud'

Death, be not proud, though some have callèd thee
    Mighty and dreadful, for thou art not so;
    For those whom thou think'st thou dost overthrow
Die not, poor Death, nor yet canst thou kill me.
From rest and sleep, which but they pictures be,
    Much pleasure – then, from thee much more must flow;
    And soonest our best men with thee do go,
Rest of their bones and soul's delivery.
Thou'rt slave to fate, chance, kings and desperate men,
    And dost with poison, war, and sickness dwell;
    And poppy or charms can make us sleep as well,
And better than thy stroke. Why swell'st thou then?
    One short sleep past, we wake eternally,
    And death shall be no more. Death, thou shalt die.

John Donne
1572–1631, b. England

John Donne's family were devout Catholics, although he grew to renounce his faith and became Dean of St Paul's (1621) – Donne's famous sermons are as fascinating as his poems. He is regarded as the founder of Metaphysical poetry – a style which explores paradox, novelty, and ingenious comparisons, and often gives the effect of a speaking voice. This particular poem is one of the 'holy sonnets' Donne wrote probably between 1610–11.

Remember

Remember me when I am gone away,
  Gone far away into the silent land;
  When you can no more hold me by the hand.
Nor I half turn to go yet turning stay.
Remember me when no more day by day
  You tell me of our future that you plann'd:
  Only remember me; you understand
It will be late to counsel then or pray.
Yet if you should forget me for a while
  And afterwards remember, do not grieve:
  For if the darkness and corruption leave
  A vestige of the thoughts that once I had,
Better by far you should forget and smile
  Than that you should remember and be sad.

Christina Rossetti

1830-1894, b. England

Christina Rossetti, like her mother and sister, was a devout High Anglican. As her life became severely restricted through continual ill health and caring for invalid relatives, she turned increasingly to her religious faith for strength and courage. In Poetical Works (published posthumously in 1904), her brother William, the editor, wrote: 'Death, as the avenue to a higher life, was contemplated by Christina Rossetti without nervousness or repulsion, even for the most part with desire . . .'

168

Tomorrow they'll be coming to get me

This isn't paranoia. This is experience.
I've watched my pals go one by one.
We used to dance all together
with our friends that have been moved
out of their homes. Now new ones have come
with their long faces. White faces.
We are getting done in for a pound of beef
a wardrobe, a letter, a roll of toilet paper.
We did mount protests. Sit-in-the-forest-
don't-budge kind of thing. But we're no match
for those big machetes. They don't care.
Basically. We're not Burnham Woods either.
We can't just up and off to a nicer spot.
Then again, we've been here hundreds of years.
Tomorrow it is another story. Chop. Tomorrow
after that, chop chop, and so it will go on
until we are all done. But then.
There will be floods like Noah never imagined.
Bright blinding lights. The earth's skin
burnt to tatters. Mark my words.
This is a dangerous game they're playing.

Jacky Kay

1961, b. Scotland

Signal Award winner Jacky Kay grew up in Glasgow and now writes plays for theatre, TV and radio, as well as composing poetry. A great admirer of Robert Burns, she sometimes uses Scottish dialect in her work. Much of her work is based on her real childhood experience, although this particular poem is written from the perspective of a threatened rainforest dweller. It comes from her first collection for children, **Two's Company** *(1992).*

'Ariel's Song' *from The Tempest*

Full fathom five thy father lies,
Of his bones are coral made;
Those are pearls that were his eyes,
Nothing of him that doth fade,
But doth suffer a sea-change
Into something rich, and strange:
Sea-nymphs hourly ring his knell –
Hark! now I hear them,
Ding-dong bell.

William Shakespeare

1564–1616, b. England

Shakespeare's play The Tempest *is full of poetry and songs. It takes place on an island in faraway seas, the home of a strange band of characters: a magician called Prospero, his daughter Miranda, a spirit called Ariel and a sad monster called Caliban. Shakespeare was alive at a time when explorers (such as Francis Drake) were being sent on dangerous voyages returning home with fantastic stories of strange animals and odd-looking people.*

170

Not Waving But Drowning

Nobody heard him, the dead man,
But still he lay moaning:
I was much further out than you thought
And not waving but drowning.

Poor chap, he always loved larking
And now he's dead
It must have been too cold for him his heart gave way,
They said.

Oh, no no no, it was too cold always
(Still the dead one lay moaning)
I was much too far out all my life
And not waving but drowning.

Stevie Smith

1902–71, b. England

Born Florence Margaret, Stevie Smith wrote three novels but is best known for her witty, humorous verse, which she often illustrated herself. The poem Not Waving But Drowning was originally published in The Observer, and lent its title to her second collection of poetry (1957). Poetry readings were very popular in the 1960s and Stevie Smith's were renowned for being particularly enjoyable.

from The Rubaiyat of Omar Khayyam

A Book of Verses underneath the Bough,
A Jug of Wine, a Loaf of Bread – and Thou
    Beside me singing in the Wilderness –
O, Wilderness were Paradise enow!

Some for the Glories of This World; and some
Sigh for the Prophet's Paradise to come;
    Ah, take the Cash, and let the Credit go,
Nor heed the rumble of a distant Drum!

Look to the blowing Rose about us – 'Lo,
Laughing,' she says, 'into the world I blow.
    At once the silken tassel of my Purse
Tear, and its Treasure on the Garden throw.'

And those who husbanded the Golden grain
And those who flung it to the winds like Rain,
    Alike to no such aureate Earth are turned
As, buried once, Men want dug up again.

The Worldly Hope men set their Hearts upon
Turns Ashes – or it prospers; and anon,
    Like Snow upon the Desert's dusty Face,
Lighting a little hour or two – is gone.

Edward Fitzgerald
1809–83, b. England

*E*dward Fitzgerald's first book appeared at the age of 40 – a biography of the Quaker poet, Bernard Barton, whose daughter he later married. His other published works were largely translations, by far the most famous being his translations of the rubais or quatrains of the 12th century Persian poet Omar Khayyam. Fitzgerald was close friends with Thakeray, Alfred and Frederick Tennyson, and Carlyle, and his many letters are fascinating.

Warning

When I am an old woman I shall wear purple
With a red hat which doesn't go, and doesn't suit me,
And I shall spend my pension on brandy and summer gloves
And satin sandals, and say we've no money for butter.
I shall sit down on the pavement when I'm tired
And gobble up samples in shops and press alarm bells
And run my stick along the public railings
And make up for the sobriety of my youth.
I shall go out in my slippers in the rain
And pick the flowers in other people's gardens
And learn to spit.

You can wear terrible shirts and grow more fat
And eat three pounds of sausages at a go
Or only bread and pickle for a week
And hoard pens and pencils and beermats and things in boxes.

But now we must have clothes that keep us dry
And pay our rent and not swear in the street
And set a good example for the children.
We must have friends to dinner and read the papers.

But maybe I ought to practise a little now?
So people who know me are not too shocked and surprised
When suddenly I am old, and start to wear purple.

Jenny Joseph
b. 1932, England

174

A popular writer for adults and children, Jenny Joseph's first collection of poems, The Unlooked-for Season (1960), won an Eric Gregory award. Joseph began her writing career as a newspaper reporter, and her sharp powers of observation enrich her poetry with the intimate detail of human life. The poem featured here celebrates the daredevil and carefree abandon that can accompany advancing years.

If

If you can keep your head when all about you
    Are losing theirs and blaming it on you,
If you can trust yourself when all men doubt you,
    But make allowance for their doubting too;
If you can wait and not be tired by waiting,
    Or being lied about, don't deal in lies,
Or being hated, don't give way to hating,
    And yet don't look too good, nor talk too wise:

If you can dream – and not make dreams your master;
    If you can think – and not make thoughts your aim;
If you can meet with Triumph and Disaster
    And treat those two impostors just the same;
If you can bear to hear the truth you've spoken
    Twisted by knaves to make a trap for fools,
Or watch the things you gave your life to, broken,
    And stoop and build 'em up with worn-out tools:

If you can make one heap of all your winnings
    And risk it on one turn of pitch-and-toss,
And lose, and start again at your beginnings
    And never breathe a word about your loss;
If you can force your heart and nerve and sinew
    To serve your turn long after they are gone,
And so hold on when there is nothing in you
    Except the Will which says to them: 'Hold on!'

If you can talk with crowds and keep your virtue,
    Or walk with Kings – nor lose the common touch,
If neither foes nor loving friends can hurt you,
    If all men count with you, but none too much;
If you can fill the unforgiving minute
    With sixty seconds' worth of distance run,
Yours is the Earth and everything that's in it,
    And – which is more – you'll be a Man, my son!

Rudyard Kipling

1865–1936, b. India

This poem was first published in *Rewards and Fairies* (1910). Thirty years later, Winston Churchill used it to encourage the population in the grim days of World War II. He cited the lines: 'If you can dream – and not make dreams your master; If you can think – and not make thoughts your aim; If you can meet with Triumph and Disaster And treat those two impostors just the same.'

'Because I could not stop for Death'

1. Because I could not stop for Death –
   He kindly stopped for me –
   The Carriage held but just Ourselves –
   And Immortality.

2. We slowly drove – He knew no haste
   And I had put away
   My labor and my leisure too,
   For His Civility –

3. We passed the School, where Children strove
   At Recess – in the Ring –
   We passed the Fields of Gazing Grain –
   We passed the Setting Sun –

4. Or rather – He passed Us –
   The Dews drew quivering and chill –
   For only Gossamer, my Gown –
   My Tippet – only Tulle –

5. We paused before a House that seemed
   A Swelling of the Ground –
   The Roof was scarcely visible –
   The Cornice – in the Ground –

6. Since then – 'tis Centuries – and yet
   Feels shorter than the Day
   I first surmised the Horses' Heads
   Were toward Eternity –

Emily Dickinson
1830–86, b. USA

Although Emily Dickinson once actively sought publication for her poems, only seven poems were published during her lifetime. She seems to have accepted that she would remain unknown as a writer, yet over the years, her work became increasingly focused on herself as a poet, a mystic love for God, a playing on the value of life, and a fascination with death and immortality.

Index of first lines and titles

First lines appear in italic